Diana Rigg

Dame Enid **Diana** Elizabeth **Rigg**, DBE, born on 20th July 1938, Doncaster, West Riding of Yorkshire, England, UK is an actress, who played Emma Peel in the TV series The Avengers (1965–68) then Olenna Tyrell in Game of Thrones (2013–17). Rigg has also had a career in theatre, including playing the title role in Medea, both in London and New York, for which she won the Tony Award for Best Actress in a Play during 1994. Diana was made a CBE in 1988 then a Dame for services to drama during 1994 .

Rigg made her professional stage debut in 1957 in The Caucasian Chalk Circle, before joining the Royal Shakespeare Company during 1959. She made her Broadway debut in a production of Abelard & Heloise in 1971. Diana's movie roles include Helena in A Midsummer Night's Dream (1968); Countess Teresa di Vicenzo, wife of James Bond, in On Her Majesty's Secret Service (1969); Lady Holiday in The Great Muppet Caper (1981) then Arlena Marshall in Evil Under the Sun (1982). Rigg won the BAFTA TV Award for Best Actress for the BBC miniseries Mother Love (1989) then an Emmy Award for her role as Mrs. Danvers in an adaptation of Rebecca (1997). Her other TV credits include You, Me and the Apocalypse (2015), Detectorists (2015), and the Doctor Who episode 'The Crimson Horror' (2013) with her daughter, Rachael Stirling.

Diana is the daughter of Louis Rigg (1903–1968) and Beryl Hilda (née Helliwell; 1908–1981), her father being a Yorkshire born railway engineer. Between the ages of 2 months and 8 years Diana lived in Bikaner, India, where her father was employed as a railway executive, having spoken Hindi as her 2nd language. She was later sent back to England to attend a boarding school, Fulneck Girls School, in a Moravian settlement near Pudsey.

Rigg hated her boarding school, where she felt like a fish out of water, but she believed that Yorkshire played a greater part in shaping her character than India did. Diana trained as an actress at the Royal Academy of Dramatic Art from 1955–57, where her classmates included Glenda Jackson and Siân Phillips.

Rigg's career in films, TV and the theatre has been wide-ranging, including roles in the Royal Shakespeare Company between 1959 - 1964. Her professional debut was as Natasha Abashwilli in the RADA production of The Caucasian Chalk Circle at the York Festival during 1957. Diana returned to the stage in the Ronald Millar play Abelard and Heloïse in London in 1970, making her Broadway debut with the play the following year, receiving the first of 3 Tony Award nominations for Best Actress in a Play. She received her 2nd nomination during 1975, for The Misanthrope. A member of the National Theatre Company at the Old Vic from 1972 to 1975, Rigg took leading roles in premiere productions of two Tom Stoppard plays, Dorothy Moore in Jumpers (National Theatre, 1972) then Ruth Carson in Night and Day (Phoenix Theatre, 1978).

Diana appeared in a musical titled Colette in 1982, based on the life of the French writer, created by Tom Jones and Harvey Schmidt, but it closed during a US tour en route to Broadway. She took a leading role in the West End production of Stephen Sondheim's musical Follies during 1987. Rigg had triumphs with roles at the Almeida Theatre in Islington in the '90s, including Medea in 1992, which transferred to the Wyndham's Theatre the following year then Broadway during 1994, for which she received the Tony Award for Best Actress. Her next was Mother Courage at the National Theatre in 1995 then Who's Afraid of Virginia Woolf? at the Almeida Theatre during 1996, which transferred to the Aldwych Theatre the following year.

Diana appeared as Violet Venable in Sheffield Theatres' production of Tennessee Williams's play Suddenly Last Summer in 2004, which transferred to the Albery Theatre. She appeared at the Wyndham's Theatre in London's West End, in a drama entitled Honour during 2006, which had a limited but successful run. Rigg appeared as Huma Rojo in the Old Vic's production of All About My Mother the next year, adapted by Samuel Adamson and based on the movie of the same title, directed by Pedro Almodóvar.

Diana appeared in The Cherry Orchard at the Chichester Festival Theatre in 2008, returning there the following year to star in Noël Coward's Hay Fever. She played Mrs. Higgins in Pygmalion at the Garrick Theatre during 2011, opposite Rupert Everett and Kara Tointon, having played Eliza Doolittle 37 years earlier at the Albery Theatre. Rigg returned to Broadway in the non-singing role of Mrs. Higgins in My Fair Lady in February 2018, saying on taking the role, "I think it's so special. When I was offered Mrs. Higgins, I thought it was just such a lovely idea". She received her 4th Tony nomination for the role.

Diana appeared in the British '60s TV series The Avengers (1961–69) opposite Patrick Macnee as John Steed, playing the secret agent Emma Peel in 51 episodes, having replaced Elizabeth Shepherd at very short notice when Shepherd was dropped from the role after filming two episodes. Rigg auditioned for the role on a whim, without ever having seen the programme. Although Diana was hugely successful in the series, she disliked the lack of privacy that it brought, not being comfortable with her position as a sex symbol. Rigg stated during 2019 that "becoming a sex symbol overnight had shocked" her, having not liked the way that she was treated by production company Associated British Corporation (ABC).

For her 2nd series Diana held out for a pay rise from £150 / week to £450, saying in 2019, when gender pay inequality was in the news that "not one woman in the industry supported me ... Neither did Patrick... but I was painted as this mercenary creature by the press, when all I wanted was equality. It's so depressing that we're still talking about the gender pay gap". Rigg didn't stay for a third year.

Patrick Macnee observed that she'd later told him that she regarded him and her driver to be her only friends on the set. On the big screen Diana became a Bond girl in On Her Majesty's Secret Service (1969), playing Tracy Bond, James Bond's only wife, opposite George Lazenby. Rigg said that she took the role hoping that she'd become better known in the US. She starred in a short-lived US sitcom titled Diana from 1973–1974.

Her other films from this period include The Assassination Bureau (1969), Julius Caesar (1970), The Hospital (1971), Theatre of Blood (1973), In This House of Brede (1975), based on the book by Rumer Godden then A Little Night Music (1977). Rigg appeared as the title character in The Marquise (1980), a TV adaptation of play by Noël Coward then the following year was in Yorkshire Television's production of Ibsen's Hedda Gabler (1981) in the title role, and as Lady Holiday in the picture The Great Muppet Caper (1981). Diana received acclaim for her performance as Arlena Marshall in the movie adaptation of Agatha Christie's Evil Under the Sun (1982), sharing barbs with her character's old rival, played by Maggie Smith.

Rigg appeared as Regan, the king's treacherous 2nd daughter, in a Granada Television production of King Lear (1983), which starred Laurence Olivier in the title role. As Lady Dedlock she costarred with Denholm Elliott in a TV version of Dickens' Bleak House (BBC, 1985) then played the Evil Queen, Snow White's evil stepmother, in the Cannon Movie Tales's film adaptation of Snow White (1987). Diana played Helena Vesey in Mother Love on the BBC during 1989, her portrayal of an obsessive mother who was prepared to do anything, even murder, to keep control of her son, winning Rigg that year's BAFTA for Best Television Actress.

She appeared in a movie adaptation for TV based on Danielle Steel's Zoya as Evgenia during 1995, the main character's grandmother. Diana appeared on television as Mrs Danvers in Rebecca (1997), winning an Emmy, as well as the PBS production Moll Flanders then starred as the amateur detective Mrs Bradley in The Mrs Bradley Mysteries. In this BBC series, first broadcast in the year 2000, Rigg played Gladys Mitchell's detective, Dame Beatrice Adela Le Strange Bradley, an eccentric old woman who worked for Scotland Yard as a pathologist. It wasn't a critical success, so didn't return for a 2nd series.

She hosted the PBS TV series Mystery!, shown in the US by PBS broadcaster WGBH from 1989 to 2003, taking over from Vincent Price, her co-star in Theatre of Blood. Diana's TV career in America has been varied, having starred in her own eponymous sitcom Diana (1973), but it wasn't a hit. She also appeared in the 2nd series of Ricky Gervais's comedy Extras, alongside Harry Potter star Daniel Radcliffe then in the picture The Painted Veil (2006).

Rigg appeared in an episode of Doctor Who in a Victorian-era based story titled 'The Crimson Horror' during 2013, alongside her daughter Rachael Stirling, Matt Smith and Jenna-Louise Coleman, which had been specially written for her and Rachael by Mark Gatiss then broadcast as part of series 7. It wasn't the first time mother and daughter had appeared in the same production, that had been in the NBC film In the Beginning (2000), but it was the first time Diana had worked with her daughter, also being the first time in her career that she'd gotten to use her Doncaster, Yorkshire, accent.

That same year, Rigg had a recurring role in the 3rd season of the HBO series Game of Thrones, portraying Lady Olenna Tyrell, a witty and sarcastic political mastermind, popularly known as the Queen of Thorns, the paternal grandmother of regular character Margaery Tyrell. Her performance was well received by critics and audiences alike, Diana receiving an Emmy nomination for Outstanding Guest Actress in a Drama Series at the 65th Primetime Emmy Awards in 2013.

Rigg reprised her part in season 4 of Game of Thrones, receiving another Guest Actress Emmy nomination during July 2014, before returning in seasons 5 and 6, in a role expanded from that in the books. Lady Olenna was killed off in the 7th season, with Diana's final performance being critically acclaimed but she said in April 2019 that she'd never watched Game of Thrones, before or after her time on the show.

Rigg lived for 8 years with director Philip Saville during the '60s, attracting attention in the tabloids when she stated that she wasn't interested in marrying the older, already-married Saville, saying she had no desire "to be respectable". Diana was married to Menachem Gueffen, an Israeli painter, born in Haifa, Palestine from 1973 until their divorce in 1976 then to Archibald Stirling, a theatrical producer and former officer in the Scots Guards, from 25th March 1982, until their divorce during 1990, after his affair with the actress Joely Richardson. Rigg had a daughter with Archibald, actress Rachael Stirling, who was born in 1977. Her first grandchild, a boy named Jack, was born during April 2017, the son of Rachael and Elbow frontman Guy Garvey.

Diana has long been an outspoken critic of feminism, saying in 1969, "Women are in a much stronger position than men". Rigg is a Patron of International Care & Relief, having been the public face of the charity's child sponsorship scheme for many years. She was also Chancellor of the University of Stirling, a ceremonial rather than executive role, being succeeded by James Naughtie when her 10-year term of office ended on 31st July 2008.

Michael Parkinson, who first interviewed Diana during 1972, described her as the most desirable woman he ever met, who "radiated a lustrous beauty". A smoker from the age of 18, Rigg was still getting through 20 cigarettes / day in 2009 but by December 2017, she'd quit after serious illness led to heart surgery, following a cardiac ablation, two months earlier. A devout Christian, Diana said : "My heart had stopped ticking during the procedure, so I was up there and the good Lord must have said, 'Send the old bag down again, I'm not having her yet!'"

Rigg said in June 2015, regarding the chemistry between Patrick Macnee and herself on The Avengers, despite her being 16 years younger: "I sort of vaguely knew Patrick Macnee, he looked kindly on me and sort of husbanded me through the first couple of episodes. After that we became equal, loved each other and sparked off each other then we'd improvise, write our own lines. They trusted us. Particularly our scenes when we were finding a dead body—I mean, another dead body. How do you get 'round that one? They allowed us to do it".

She also said about the improvisation of the dialogue: "Not for an instant, no. Well, when I say improvising, Pat and I would sit down to work out approximately what we'd say. It wasn't sort of...who's the American duo? Mike Nichols and Elaine May. It was definitely not that". Asked if she'd ever stayed in touch with Macnee in an interview published two days before his death, decades after they were reunited for one last time on her short-lived American series Diana : "You'll always be close to somebody that you worked with very intimately for so long, and you become really fond of each other but we haven't seen each other for a very, very long time".

Filmography

Film

Year	Title	Role	Notes
1968	A Midsummer Night's Dream	Helena	
1969	Mini-Killers	short film	
	The Assassination Bureau	Sonya Winter	
	On Her Majesty's Secret Service	Contessa Teresa "Tracy" Draco di Vicenzo Bond	

1970   Julius Caesar   Portia

1971   The Hospital   Barbara Drummond

1973   Theatre of Blood   Edwina Lionheart

1977   A Little Night Music   Countess Charlotte
Mittelheim

1981   The Great Muppet Caper   Lady Holiday

1982   Evil Under the Sun   Arlena Marshall

1986   The Worst Witch   Miss Hardbroom

1987   Snow White   The Evil Queen, Snow White's evil
stepmother

1994   A Good Man in Africa   Chloe Fanshawe

1999   Parting Shots   Lisa

2005   Heidi   Grandmamma

2006   The Painted Veil   Mother Superior

2015   The Honourable Rebel   Narrator

2017   BreatheLady Neville

2020   Last Night in Soho   Miss Collins   Post-
production

Television

Year   Title   Role   Notes

1959   A Midsummer Night's Dream   Bit part   TV film

1963   The Sentimental Agent Francy Wilde   Episode: 'A Very Desirable Plot'

1964   Festival Adriana Episode: 'The Comedy of Errors'

Armchair Theatre   Anita Fender   Episode: 'The Hothouse'

1965   ITV Play of the Week   Bianca   Episode: 'Women Beware Women'

1965–68   The Avengers   Emma Peel   Main role (51 episodes)

1970   ITV Saturday Night Theatre   Liz Jardine
        Episode: 'Married Alive'

1973–74   Diana   Diana Smythe   Main role (15 episodes)

1974   Affairs of the Heart   Grace Gracedew
        Episode: 'Grace'

1975   In This House of Brede PhilippaTV film

The Morecambe & Wise Show   Nell Gwynne   sketch in Christmas Show

1977   Three Piece Suite   Various Regular role (6 episodes)

1979   Oresteia   Clytemnestra   TV miniseries

1980   The Marquise   Eloise   TV film

1981   Hedda Gabler   Hedda Gabler   TV film

1982   Play of the Month   Rita Allmers   Episode:
Little Eyolf

Witness for the Prosecution   Christine Vole   TV film

1983   King Lear   Regan   TV film

1985   Bleak House   Lady Honoria Dedlock TV miniseries

1986   The Worst Witch   Miss Constance Hardbroom
TV film

1987   A Hazard of Hearts   Lady Harriet Vulcan   TV
film

1989   The Play on One   Lydia   Episode:
'Unexplained Laughter'

Mother Love   Helena Vesey TV miniseries

British Academy Television Award for Best Actress

Broadcast Press Guild Award for Best Actress

1992   Mrs. 'Arris Goes to Paris Mme. Colbert   TV film

1993   Road to Avonlea   Lady Blackwell   Episode: 'The
Disappearance'

Running Delilah Judith   TV film

Screen Two   Baroness Frieda von Stangel   Episode:
'Genghis Cohn'

Nominated – CableACE Award for Best Supporting Actress in a
Miniseries or Movie

1994   Genghis Cohn   Frieda von Stangel   TV film

1995   Zoya   Evgenia   TV film

The Haunting of Helen Walker   Mrs. Grose   TV film

1996   The Fortunes and Misfortunes of Moll Flanders   Mrs. Golightly   TV film

Samson and Delilah   Mara   TV film

1997   Rebecca   Mrs. Danvers   TV miniseries

Primetime Emmy Award for Outstanding Supporting Actress in a Miniseries or a Movie

1998   The American   Madame de Bellegarde   TV film

1998–2000   The Mrs Bradley Mysteries   Mrs. Adela Bradley Main role (5 episodes)

2000   In the Beginning   Mature Rebeccah   TV film

2001   Victoria & Albert   Baroness Lehzen   TV miniseries

Nominated – Primetime Emmy Award for Outstanding Supporting Actress in a Miniseries or a Movie

2003   Murder in Mind Jill Craig   Episode: 'Suicide'

Charles II: The Power and the Passion   Queen Henrietta Maria   TV miniseries

2006   Extras   herself   Episode: 'Daniel Radcliffe'

2013–17   Game of Thrones   Olenna Tyrell   18 episodes

Nominated – Primetime Emmy Award for Outstanding Guest Actress in a Drama Series (2013, 2014, 2015, 2018)

Nominated – Critics' Choice Television Award for Best Guest Performer in a Drama Series (2013, 2014)

2013   Doctor Who   Mrs. Winifred Gillyflower
Episode: 'The Crimson Horror'

2015, 2017   Penn Zero: Part-Time Hero   Mayor Pink
Panda (voice)   3 episodes

Detectorists   Veronica   6 episodes

2015   You, Me and the Apocalypse   Sutton   5
episodes

Professor Branestawm Returns Lady Pagwell   TV film

2017   Victoria Duchess of Buccleuch   9 episodes

2019   The Snail and The Whale   Narrator   short
TV film

2020   Black Narcissus Mother Dorothea   upcoming
miniseries

Theatre

Year   Title   Role   Notes

1957   The Caucasian Chalk Circle   Natella Abashwili
        Theatre Royal, York Festival

1964   King Lear   Cordelia   Royal Shakespeare
Company (European/US Tour)

1966   Twelfth Night   Viola Royal Shakespeare Company

1970   Abelard and Heloise   Heloise   Wyndham's
Theatre, London

1971   Abelard and Heloise   Heloise   Brooks
Atkinson Theatre, New York

1972   Macbeth   Lady Macbeth   Old Vic Theatre,
London

1972   Jumpers   Dorothy Moore Old Vic Theatre, London

1973   The Misanthrope   Célimène   Old Vic Theatre,
London

1974   Pygmalion   Eliza Doolittle   Albery Theatre,
London

1975   The Misanthrope   Célimène   St. James
Theatre, New York

1978   Night and Day   Ruth Carson   Phoenix
Theatre, London

1982   Colette   Colette   US national tour

1983   Heartbreak House   Lady Ariadne UtterwordTheatre
Royal Haymarket, London

1985   Little Eyolf   Rita Allmers   Lyric Theatre,
Hammersmith, London

14

1985   Antony and Cleopatra   Cleopatra   Chichester
Festival Theatre, UK

1986   WildfireBess   Theatre Royal, Bath & Phoenix
Theatre, London

1987   Follies   Phyllis Rogers Stone Shaftesbury Theatre,
London

1990   Love Letters   Melissa   Stage Door Theatre, San
Francisco

1992   Putting It Together   Old Fire Station Theatre, Oxford

1992   Berlin Bertie   Rosa   Royal Court Theatre,
London

1992   Medea   Medea   Almeida Theatre, London

1993   Medea   Medea   Wyndham's Theatre, London

1994   Medea   Medea   Longacre Theatre, New York

1995   Mother Courage and Her Children   Mother
Courage   National Theatre, London

1996   Who's Afraid of Virginia Woolf   Martha   Almeida
Theatre, London

1997   Who's Afraid of Virginia Woolf   Martha Aldwych
Theatre, London

1998   Phaedra   Phaedra   Almeida at the Albery
Theatre, London & BAM in Brooklyn

1998   Britannicus   Agrippina   Almeida at the Albery
Theatre, London & BAM in Brooklyn

2001   Humble Boy   Flora Humble   National Theatre, London

2002   The Hollow Crown   International Tour: New Zealand, Australia, Stratford-upon-Avon, UK

2004   Suddenly, Last Summer Violet Venable Albery Theatre, London

2006   Honour Honour Wyndham's Theatre, London

2007   All About My Mother   Huma Rojo Old Vic Theatre, London

2008   The Cherry Orchard   Ranyevskaya Chichester Festival Theatre, UK

2009   Hay Fever   Judith Bliss   Chichester Festival Theatre, UK

2011   Pygmalion   Mrs. Higgins   Garrick Theatre, London

2018   My Fair Lady   Mrs. Higgins Vivian Beaumont Theatre, New York

Honours, awards and nominations

Rigg received honorary degrees from the University of Stirling during 1988, the University of Leeds in 1992 then London South Bank University during 1996.

Diana was made a Commander of the Order of the British Empire (CBE) in the New Year Honours of 1988 then a Dame

Commander of the Order of the British Empire (DBE) for services to drama in the Birthday Honours of 1994.

Rigg received the Will Award in 2014, presented by the Shakespeare Theatre Company, along with Stacy Keach and John Hurt.

To mark 50 years of Emma Peel, the BFI (British Film Institute) screened an episode of The Avengers on 25th October 2015, followed by an onstage interview with Diana about her time on the TV series.

Year	Award	Category	Work	Result
1967	Emmy Award	Best Actress in a Drama Series	The Avengers	nominated
1968				nominated
1970	Laurel Award	Female New Face	The Assassination Bureau	nominated
1971	Tony Award	Best Actress in a Play	Abelard and Heloise	nominated
1972	Golden Globe	Best Supporting Actress (motion picture)	The Hospital	nominated
1975	Tony Award	Best Actress in a Play	The Misanthrope	nominated
	Drama Desk Award	Outstanding Actress in a Play		nominated
	Emmy Award	Best Actress in a TV Movie	In This House of Brede	nominated

1990   BAFTA TV Award   Best Actress   Mother Love
        Won

Broadcasting Press Guild Award Best Actress   Won

1992   Evening Standard Award   Best Actress
Medea Won

1994   Olivier Award   Best Actress nominated

Drama Desk Award   Outstanding Actress in a Play
        nominated

Tony Award   Best Actress in a Play Won

1996   CableACE Award   Supporting Actress in a Movie
or Miniseries   Screen Two (1985) – episode 'Genghis Cohn'
        nominated

Olivier Award   Best Actress   Mother Courage
nominated

Evening Standard Award   Best Actress   Mother
Courage and Who's Afraid of Virginia Woolf   Won

1997   Olivier Award   Best Actress Who's Afraid of Virginia
Woolf   nominated

Emmy Award   Best Supporting Actress in a Miniseries or TV
Movie   Rebecca   Won

1999   Olivier Award   Best Actress Britannicus and Phedre
        nominated

2000   Special BAFTA Award   non-competitive John Steed's
partners   shared with Honor Blackman, Linda Thorson and

Joanna Lumley. The Avengers (and The New Avengers)
        Awarded

2002   Emmy Award   Best Supporting Actress in a
Miniseries or TV Movie Victoria & Albert   nominated

2013   Critics' Choice Television Award Best Guest Performer in
a Drama Series Game of Thrones   nominated

Emmy Award   Outstanding Guest Actress in a Drama Series
        nominated

2014   Critics' Choice Television Award Best Guest Performer in
a Drama Series nominated

Emmy Award   Outstanding Guest Actress in a Drama Series
        nominated

2015   Emmy Award   Outstanding Guest Actress in a Drama
Series   nominated

2018   Drama Desk Award   Best Featured Actress in a
Musical My Fair Lady   nominated

Tony Award   Best Featured Actress in a Musical
        nominated

Emmy Award   Outstanding Guest Actress in a Drama Series
        Game of Thrones   nominated

2019   Canneseries   Variety Icon Award   N/A   Won

No Turn Unstoned, a collection of scathing theatrical reviews
collected by Rigg was first published in 1982.

Dame Diana Rigg is a lady whose enduring charms have cut across the generations with almost boundless ease, it being the role of Emma Peel in the '60s TV show The Avengers that she'd be forever famous for. As the all-action, cat-suited Mrs. Peel, she was a resounding hit, as much for her wonderfully English performance as for her undoubtedly resonant sex appeal. Although she hit a peak during the late '60s - early '70s, but had found an Indian summer over recent years, with books and acting roles, including 'The Mrs Bradley Mysteries', leading to even more plaudits. On top of this, the timeless beauty had just triumphed in a poll of the sexiest women of all time.

"My father was a railway engineer who got a good job in India, so although I was born in Yorkshire I spent the first 8 years of my life out there but Yorkshire really formed my character. I get straight to the point, saying what I feel. I can't help it, it's genetic. That's my excuse anyway. I was sent back home to go to boarding school. I hated it – that left me feeling disenfranchised most of my life, as if I didn't belong anywhere. I might as well have said I wanted to go on the game when I told the headmistress I wanted to be an actress.

When I joined the RSC I was, literally, a spear-carrier. I had a walk-on part, watching the likes of Dame Edith Evans and Laurence Olivier who were in the company. What a training. Becoming a sex symbol overnight [in The Avengers] shocked me. I didn't know how to handle it, I kept all the unopened fan mail in the boot of my car, because I didn't know how to respond but thought it was rude to throw it away. Then my mother became my secretary, replying to the really inappropriate ones saying: 'My daughter's far too old for you. Go take a cold shower!'

Not one woman in the industry supported me when I demanded more money after finding out the cameraman on The Avengers was paid a lot more than me. Neither did Patrick [Macnee, Rigg's co-star], although I never held it against him, I adored him but I was painted as this mercenary creature by the press, when all I wanted was equality. It's so depressing that we're still talking about the gender pay gap.

Yes I have a dark side, doesn't everyone? I've played a lot of evil, ball-breaking women and if you're honest, you'll just drag up from the depths all the times you've hated or felt passionately about something and play it. I turned 80 last year when I was playing Mrs Higgins in My Fair Lady on Broadway. I gave a huge party, inventing my own cocktail called Diana's Dynamite – Prosecco with Cointreau – which got everyone hammered.

When I appeared nude in a play on Broadway in the early '70s, a nasty little critic said I was built like a brick mausoleum with insufficient flying buttresses. He should have seen me after the menopause, there was no shortfall then! It was devastating at the time. It wasn't my decision to have Lady Olenna killed off in Game of Thrones. I'd love to have stayed on. Thank God I didn't die on a toilet like Charles Dance's character".

Dame Diana Rigg may've being turning 70 but she still drove a Mercedes sports car, smoked 20 fags / day and swore by a bottle of Merlot before bedtime. The spirit of Emma Peel lived on. A tall, broad-shouldered woman with a straight spine and a thick bob of dyed blonde hair was standing under a lowboughed tree in the Chelsea Physic Garden, of which she was a member . It was Diana, with her head in the branches, emerging picking petals from her hair, looking to the overcast sky, saying, 'This flat light is very good for a woman of my age'.

Although Rigg looked her age in a way that Julie Christie, her fellow '60s sex symbol didn't, her strong features - retroussé nose and high cheekbones, down-turned eyes and mouth - were still softly handsome. Dressed in pin-stripe trousers and a red jacket, with only a suggestion of make-up, Diana seemed comfortable with herself. Too dignified to be vain. Not really the cosmetic surgery type, despite having had the wrinkles around her eyes removed when she was 44.

A decade earlier, when Rigg was in Ted Hughes's adaptation of Racine's Phèdre, folk were still allowed to smoke in restaurants, which she made the most of. She still smoked a pack a day, but was relaxed about the smoking ban in public places. Diana walked around the corner to Foxtrot Oscar restaurant, because they mixed a good bloody Mary there, talking about Chekhov's The Cherry Orchard.

She'd just finished a run of the play at Chichester - 'Got a right old buffeting from the critics, but I loved it and we played to 74% capacity, so up yours critics' - being about to head off for the summer to her place in France, south-east of Bordeaux. There Rigg would cook for friends, read, listen to music and swim naked in her pool. At night she listened to the owls. She felt freer there than in her Kensington flat, more at ease. Because she'd always despised herself for not speaking fluent French, Diana took herself off to the Lycée to learn it. 'I'm still chary of speaking French outside France, though'.

At the restaurant she ordered her bloody Mary, saying that the mayor of the French village had asked if he could hunt wild boar in the land around her house. 'So they all came in their vans with their dogs, blew their horns then killed two adult wild boar, mother and father. Very medieval. Carried them out of the wood on a stick, but one of the young boars escaped then took refuge under my neighbour's bed. The saying in the village was that she had the pig under her bed, whereas normally he's on top of it'. Rigg laughed at the joke, being in a good mood, an end-of-term frivolity but could be glacial when she wanted to be.

She said, 'I don't normally drink at lunchtime. I'm not saying that defensively, I just don't and in the evening I never drink before 6pm, an old habit acquired from my father'. Diana made up for it after that, though, believing in 'red before bed'. A cheap bottle of Chilean merlot gave one the best night's sleep in the world, she reckoned, like being hit over the head, waking up 10 hrs later, feeling like a spring lamb.

Although Rigg described herself as 'hopelessly un-neurotic,' believing that she might be a better actress if she were more neurotic, Diana did have a sudden, explosive temper, and the angrier she got the more articulate she became. Rigg was intolerant of queue-jumpers, litter-droppers and bad-mannered people generally. When driving, she'd roll down her window then yell, 'Thank you!' to folk she'd let into a line of traffic. The waitress got a taste of this sharpness when she appeared saying, 'I'm sorry to interrupt, but I'd like to talk you through the specials on the menu'. 'I think we can read. 'Thank you so much,' Diana responded.

'But they change each day,' the waitress said, staggering back slightly. When the waitress left, Rigg said of her shortness with folk that with her, things had to be said, being no good at bottling up her feelings, although she was good at saying 'sorry', never sulking. There were clips of Diana on YouTube ranging from her appearances on Parkinson - on one of which she said that her greatest pleasure in life came from biting her baby's bottom - to scenes from The Avengers, the TV series as synonymous with the '60s as were the Mini and the Beatles. The shows were psychedelic, with surreal humour - Rigg would end a fight scene by picking up her knitting.

'Oh yes, my daughter sends me YouTube clips. Not of me. Funny stuff. It all sounds like rubbish the stuff they have of me. It's a horrible thought that they're on there. I'm also a mouse pad and a screen-saver. Am I supposed to be flattered? All those old images of me floating across the screen, the terrible chasm of what you were and what you are. I know who I am, but these people who see me as I was then don't.

There's always one thing that turns you into an icon, an iconic image, in my case a catsuit but the icon 40 years later doesn't really want to know, because it's not relevant to me. Some of those early photographs of me might as well be sepia. It's always thought that I disclaim TV and am too theatre, but the truth is The Avengers bores me now. I was grateful, because it catapulted me into stage stardom. It was good. I'm not ashamed of it, but I only did it for two years'.

The leather catsuit was 'a total nightmare'; it took 45 minutes to get it unzipped. Like struggling in and out of a wetsuit. Once Diana got into the jersey catsuits, they were easy to wear but she had to watch for baggy knees. Nothing worse. At Rada she'd trained as a classical actress then afterwards joined the Royal Shakespeare Company. It sounded like she planned to use TV as a way of boosting her stage career?

'Not at all. I left the RSC not knowing what I was going to do, ending up getting a telly job with Harry Corbett, only because the director's wife had been cast opposite him then had to drop out. After that, my agent put me up for The Avengers but I didn't have a telly, so I didn't know what it was. When it came out, I was suddenly famous. It was startling! From being anonymous, I was mobbed!".

Once Diana had to hide in the lavatory at the Motor Show, while in Germany police resorted to batons to hold back the fans. Slavering fan mail was another problem, so she'd get her mother, Beryl, to field the letters. The replies were usually along the lines of: 'Those aren't very nice thoughts and besides, my daughter is too old for you. I suggest you take a run around the block'. Folk still sent her Avengers photos to sign, but she refused because, 'I feel such a phony. That's not me. That's another person. Fame was different then. Nowadays people court fame, Big Brother-type fame; in those days we didn't know how to court fame. There weren't the channels to court fame, the publicists. I just hope the people getting their 15 minutes now are putting their money in the building society'.

Was fame hollow? Rigg shook her head. 'I'm not the best person to ask, because whatever form it's taken for me, it has always been attached to my career. I've always tried to avoid any vestige of it touching my private life. It has always been separate. I step into a character in my public life. People who don't make that distinction are dooooomed'. This was a trait of hers: Diana stretched her vowels elastically but not camply; her voice being far too deep, smoky and unhurried for that. 'There's still that small centre of me that's never been touched by fame, never photographed, written about or discussed. So when I sit next to a stranger at a dinner party and they feel they know something about me, I know they don't'.

In retrospect, Rigg wished she'd allowed herself to enjoy fame more than she had. 'I should've handled it better. Had more fun. Not naughty fun but just... I sometimes think, when I look back on those days: 'Why didn't I have more confidence? Why didn't I know I was pretty good-looking? It's probably to do with my Yorkshire upbringing. Always thinking that people might be saying, 'Who does she think she is?"

Diana was born in Doncaster during 1938, but her parents were based in India, so she was taken back there after her birth. Her father, Louis Rigg, was a railway engineer who worked for the Maharaja of Bikaner, Ganga Singh. When Diana was shipped back to a gloomy Yorkshire boarding school in 1945, she felt like a fish out of water. Still, Yorkshire, she believed, played a much greater part in shaping her character than India had. It was a tradition in her household that you always had to have a slice of bread and butter without jam before you could have one with. Very Yorkshire, that.

Did Diana keep a diary? 'I don't but I wish I did, because the past is pretty unknown to me. I've so lived for the present that I can't remember the details. Smells and sounds can transport me then I remember. I don't keep memorabilia or photograph albums'. Her daughter, Rachael Stirling, was also an actress, one with a successful career, having starred in Tipping the Velvet. She looked and sounded like her mother. Had it been inevitable that she'd follow Rigg into acting? 'Her dad and I did say, 'Here we go. Fairly inevitable', but we said she must go to uni first, so she read history of art at Edinburgh'.

Was there any rivalry between mother and daughter? 'No, I don't think so. I feel more that the baton has been handed on. She doesn't use my surname, but she does look very like me'. Diana had given up working to raise her daughter; would she recommend that Rachael did the same if she had children? 'The work-life balance, you mean? I wouldn't advise her on anything, she'll do it her way. I might take over the baby if she's away. The world has changed mightily; in my mother's day you were made to feel guilty if you went out. Now everyone is left to work it out for themselves. Actually, acting was quite compatible with motherhood. I could take her to school when doing theatre. The evening was a problem, obviously but I could always put her to bed when I was doing a film or TV. I don't think my profession made any difference with her, though. My divorce? I'm not sure'.

Rigg's first marriage was during 1973 to Menahem Gueffen, an Israeli painter; her first divorce coming 3 years later. Diana married again in 1982 to a Scottish landowner, Archie Stirling, having had Rachael at the age of 39. The marriage broke up during 1990, after Archie had an affair with the actress Joely Richardson but she'd stayed on good terms with her former husband.

Rigg had previously said, 'I'm slightly aghast that you see before you a twice-divorced woman. I'm shocked. It's not how I saw myself, how I imagined things would work out, not what I believe in' but seemed to have become more at ease with the idea. When she was young, Diana said, women were considered incomplete without a husband, it having taken her many years to come to the tranquil conclusion that life could be completely without a man after all.

Rigg seemed to know herself well, understanding what made her tick, being unsentimental and matter-of-fact about herself. Diana thought she was probably quite 'anal' - actually, that's what her daughter thought but she went along with it. Her greatest fear was being 'a dithering, dribbling old bag, having to rely on help for everything'. Rigg's greatest disappointment was her film career - 'or lack of - but it's too late now'. The single thing that would improve the quality of her life would be to no longer have creaking joints: in the Stephen Sondheim musical Follies, in 1987, there was an 11-minute tap routine in high heels that permanently damaged her knees.

Diana seemed to be regarded by audience and critics alike as the most daring, intelligent and inspired tragedienne on the London and New York stage but it wasn't until she was in her 50s that she hit her stride, playing 3 award-winning leads in succession: Medea (1992-94); Mother Courage (1995) and Who's Afraid of Virginia Woolf (1996). Rigg's performance as Medea was a career high, having won a London Evening Standard Theatre Award and Tony Award for Best Actress. In it Diana played a vengeful wife who killed her estranged husband's children. Coincidentally, she'd just separated from her real husband.

In Phèdre, Rigg played the queen who fell in love with her stepson, only to find that her husband was still alive. Jealousy induced her to send him to his death, but her conscience forced her to admit her guilt before dying herself. 'With Phèdre it was typical Ted [Hughes] - muscular, strong writing - there's nothing

Ancient Greek wafty about it. It grabs you like a pair of eagle's claws. It was a huge privilege working with him.

He died during the run of the play. The night he died, we were playing it. Such poignancy - because he knew he was dying but he said to the cast, "I go to bed happy, because Phèdre is on stage'. He'd been so attacked by the feminists who blamed him for Sylvia's suicide. They felt he'd driven her to it by his infidelity. He was like an oak and I can quite see why women threw themselves at him. His poetic soul and that wonderful voice that came from his boots'.

Diana's own soul was pretty poetic, saying she was easily moved by the thought of young men fighting then dying for their country. Whenever she visited First World War battlefields she was reduced to tears. 'They're so silent, hardly any birdsong, big open fields, it's as if nature is paying reverence'. The news images of Union flag-draped coffins coming out of RAF transporter planes filled her with terrible despair and anger. Rigg joined the march against the war in Iraq, saying that she felt betrayed by Blair. 'Did he seduce me? Yes. He, generally speaking, courted my profession but I now disavow'.

Her father was a Conservative, as was her brother, a retired RAF Harrier test pilot. Diana was a crossbencher. 'I wish I could feel sorry for Gordon Brown, but I can't. He was the understudy who got the role but didn't understand it. Didn't know what to do with it. He didn't learn his lines or know his moves. I heard an alternative comedian say that even when Gordon smiles he looks like he's sh--ting a sea anemone, and that's about right. The breathing? It's a tic. A habit. He inhales and his bottom lip goes with it. He could easily see an acting coach and get rid of it, but I imagine he's too busy with other things'.

Rigg was a big Barack Obama fan, believing that John McCain was too old for the job. 'I know I should be saying the opposite, because I'm the same age as him, but I do think his age will make a difference. At 70, you aren't as physically robust as you were. I don't think your mental capacities are as good as they were. The President should be a younger man, with older advisers'.' She'd said a decade earlier that she'd intended to get a pensioner's bus pass. Had she? Actually, Diana said with a quick smile, she drove.

She'd been attacked by the Daily Mail as 'embittered' during 2002, having gone into retirement, so the paper claimed, living 'the life of a recluse' in France. The article was accompanied by a grim photograph of Rigg clutching a baguette, the caption reading: 'Shopping for one'. She'd been followed to her remote village then secretly photographed. Diana sued the newspaper for libel, winning £38,000 damages, which she donated to charity.

That said, she didn't quite enjoy silence and her own company. Rigg was still a keen fly-fisher, a solitary sport. 'I don't have a river any more. I did have when I was married, on my husband's estate. Now I just fish whenever I'm invited anywhere. I'm a fishing tart'. Diana was still the chancellor of Sterling university, though she was standing down that year. 'I'm not an academic, but I would've loved to have been one. I love the dinners with professors. You learn all sorts of things. I can tell you all about the mites that attack salmon. I can even tell you what happens in the lochs with the mounds of fish excrement'.

The life of an actress had never been secure, Rigg said, because they never really knew from one year to the next what they'd be doing. 'The grave danger is to fall into the trap of thinking you cease to exist if you no longer have a job. Obviously, economics has a bearing on this but you must fill your life with as many alternatives as possible to your job, because without that you're going to be an empty vessel'. So what did Diana have lined up next? 'Nothing next, but I still exist'.

Afterwards, a woman called out my name. It was Rigg in the driving seat of a new-looking, sky-blue Mercedes sports car, asking if I wanted a lift anywhere? A taxi arrived then she gave an ironic salute goodbye, a very Emma Peel moment. Diana was wearing sunglasses, while holding a cigarette in her hand, looking like the coolest 70-year-old you'd ever see.

Diana Rigg, famous for playing Emma Peel in the '60s series The Avengers then nearly 50 years later for ruling as Olenna Tyrell on HBO's wildly popular Game of Thrones, had always been a distinguished classical stage actress. Taking on the non-singing role of Mrs. Higgins in My Fair Lady, Rigg was truly delighted to return to Broadway, where she'd had great success, having won a Tony Award for playing the title role in Medea in 1994. Sipping Prosecco whiloe chatting about fishing "I caught a 24 1/2-inch salmon. Don't forget that half inch!", Diana was in her element, being back on the Great White Way.

Why had Rigg wanted to return to Broadway?

"I think it's so special. When I was offered Mrs. Higgins, I thought it was just such a lovely idea. I love that Americans celebrate theatre so much more than English people do. Our English audiences are good, but in New York, everybody knows

31

if you're in a success. It's so sweet. The girlies who're serving you in the shops say, 'Oh, I hear you're in such and such'. The whole of New York seems to enjoy a hit".

Diana had played Mrs. Higgins as well as Eliza Doolittle in Pygmalion. How was that informing her for this latest production?

"Having played Eliza—it was such a long time ago that it's completely different now. I mean, the attitude toward women has changed mightily, so I played Eliza in my time for my time, the time has changed, now Lauren [Ambrose] is playing it for her time. As for Mrs. Higgins, I've played her twice. It's a lovely part; it's a supporting part. She supports Eliza when not everybody is doing so, it's not just because she's sympathetic, I think it's because she's emancipated. She's a pretty emancipated woman herself".

Some adjectives used to describe Mrs. Higgins in My Fair Lady were: elegant, opinionated, refined, so was it a stretch for Rigg?

"Not a stretch, but I think I'm older than she's normally played".

How had the cast bonded?

"Oh, they're just lovely. Really welcoming and nice. I'm not the only English person: Harry [Hadden-Paton] is as well, so is Colonel Pickering [Allan Corduner]. I come from a very democratic theatrical background. I started with the Royal Shakespeare Company, so I believe in total democracy of the theatre and that we all depend upon each other, we all need each other, so there should be absolutely no hierarchy at all".

Was Diana feeling maternal toward Harry Hadden-Paton, who played Henry Higgins?

"Yes, very! He's adorable. If you have a bit of a thought about the characters—the two of them together—Mr. Higgins isn't mentioned. So, I suspect that she's brought him up on her own and is partially responsible for the man he is now".

Harry was known for being on The Crown, and Rigg was appearing in Victoria. Did they both have an affinity for the royal family?

"We haven't discussed it. Isn't it interesting? Well, his take is completely different, of course. I mean, I'm way back".

Had Diana seen him on The Crown?

"No, I haven't. I'm not a great viewer of TV series. I never see myself. It's documentaries that I like watching on television".

So, once Rigg filmed something she didn't go back to watch it?

"No. Never!"

From The Avengers to Game of Thrones, Diana had been a part of programmes that folk absolutely loved.

"It's very nice to meet people so many years after The Avengers. Women who say that Emma Peel really helped them in their lives to define or discover themselves or whatever. She was ahead of her time. I talk about her, because I played her, but I wasn't responsible for her—I didn't write her. I inherited that and I have a sense that with Game of Thrones, the fan base, if you like, is young and I'm very pleased about that because it's lovely to have generations who like your work".

Which of Rigg's characters was she most recognized for on the street?

"I'm not recognized on the street".

Really? Diana was unmistakable!

"I'm grateful for it".

What memories did Rigg have of being on Broadway.

"Oh, it was wonderful. Let me think. First time around, I was in Abelard and Heloise then the 2nd time was The Misanthrope. It was a qualified success—not a big hit then the 3rd time was with Medea, a great success, which was so wonderful when you think it was a 2000-year-old play. I remember I desperately wanted Euripides' name up in lights. I asked the producers if we could please have them up in lights, because I thought this is historic. A sellout play that is 2000 years old, and it's Euripides! but they refused to put his name in lights, because they thought it would put people off, this sort of strange Greek name up there. So, then I offered—although I wasn't earning that much money—to pay to have his name in lights but they still said no".

"Never ever drink before a show. Ever. That's forbidden. Or during but afterwards, pop goes the Prosecco!".

Well, at least Diana got to make a point of thanking Euripides in her Tony acceptance speech.

"Yes, well I just love the history of the theatre. I love the fact that our profession, which goes back longer than the Bible—not the Old Testament, but definitely the new—it predates Christ. There's been so much about it that has fed our humanity, given people hope. It has also opened people's minds to the complexities of the human condition. It's a brilliant, wonderful profession. I can get boring about it".

Rigg was with the Royal Shakespeare Company, had great success as Emma Peel in The Avengers then returned to the theatre. How important was it to her to always come back to the stage?

"It's a good question. The first thing I did, having established myself as an actress on the screen in The Avengers, was to go back to the Royal Shakespeare Company, put bums on seats to make money. Really it was because Peter Hall, who was then head of the Royal Shakespeare, heard that I was leaving to do TV then said, 'Oh, she'll waste herself on television and films' but he was so wrong, because TV and movies feed theatre. It's total inversion. People thought that it would take away from theatre, but it doesn't, time and again established actors and actresses, certainly in England, go back to the theatre".

There Diana was, on stage with folk who were theatre actors but had also made their names in television.

"Yes, and it's a justification, actually, of success on TV. When I first began, television was looked down on—you were sort of kind of demeaning yourself a bit. You're being paid a great deal more money for being on TV, and maybe you're being a bit mercenary by playing on television but now TV works for the theatre, as such being very valuable in this day and age. Now, of course, we have—I don't know if you have it in America—we have films of theatre and of shows and of opera and ballet, and people pour into the theatres to see what's on the West End, because they haven't got the money to get on a train to see it. They get to see an absolute brilliant filmed theatre piece".

In My Fair Lady, Mrs. Higgins didn't have a song.

"Thank God!. I'd empty the theatre if I had a song".

Come on. Rigg had performed in musicals!

"I've sung before, but I mean, it's too late now. Really".

If Mrs. Higgins had a song, what would its title be?

"What would it be? Oh. 'Take Me as You See Me'".

Was it true that Diana had Prosecco in her contract for Victoria, as one of her co-stars had speculated?

"No, I don't. I pay for it!. Somebody got it wrong. Can you imagine the producers buying me Prosecco? They wouldn't for an instant! I buy it and there's a dear man who's been driving me around whose boot is clinking all the time, because I give wardrobe a bottle, I give makeup a bottle. I mean, I can't just have a bottle in my caravan. You've got to spread the word, which is what I do".

Rigg shared what she enjoyed?

"Yes! I think people are a little bit more cautious in America about drinking, but in England we always have booze in our dressing rooms. Always. Never ever drink before a show. Ever. That's forbidden. Or during, but afterwards, pop goes the Prosecco".

Well, cheers to Diana.

"Cheers, and thank you for providing this Prosecco".

As Game of Thrones returned for its final series, Dame Diana Rigg - aka Olenna Tyrell - looked back on her time with the hit

HBO show. She may've had many of the best lines on Game of Thrones, but Dame Rigg said she hadn't watched the series 'before or since' she'd appeared in it. Accepting a special award at that year's Canneseries TV festival in France, Diana said she 'hadn't got a clue' about what was happening on the show.

Olenna had left at the end of the previous series by drinking poison - a death scene she said was 'just wonderful'. Olenna Tyrell made her final appearance in Game of Thrones the year before. "She does it with dignity and wit, and wit isn't often in final death scenes," said Rigg, who'd celebrate her 81st birthday during July 2019. The young Diana became famous in the '60s for playing Emma Peel in TV series The Avengers. Being offered Tyrell during 2013, she said, had echoed the circumstances of her first starring role.

"They just called my agent. The world turns full circle, because just like with The Avengers, I wasn't watching Game of Thrones, so had absolutely no idea of its influence in the world. It was a job, they sent me a script then I thought 'I can do this'. "Interestingly enough, they tested me very early on. One of my earliest scenes was incredibly difficult, listing all the things my marching army would need. It went on forever, talking about the sheep, the cows and the soldiers. I read that then thought, 'these guys are testing an old actress to see if she can get it into her head. I thought, 'I'm going to do it in one take' then I did".

Rigg was also known for playing Tracy, the only woman who became Mrs James Bond, in the picture, On Her Majesty's Secret Service (1969). Given the choice though, she'd choose Olenna every time. "I love playing bad characters. They're so much more interesting than good. There are some actors who don't like to play bad; they like to be liked. I love to be disliked.

Olenna had the best lines, they were very kind with their scripts".

The issue of pay equality in the film industry had been highlighted, not least by the revelation that Michelle Williams was paid a fraction of what Mark Wahlberg earned for reshooting scenes in All the Money in the World. Diana was highly supportive of Williams and her backing for the US Paycheck Fairness Act, having discovered while working on The Avengers that she was being paid less than one of its cameramen.

"I remember thinking, 'something's very wrong here. When I complained publicly, the newspapers got hold of it, I was represented as a mercenary young woman stepping out of line and demanding money. I was lonely as well, because no one supported me. I did get more money, but thereafter I was labelled as go-getting and 'hard' - which was unfair because I wasn't. The fight goes on. I wonder if anyone's done a survey as to whether people go to watch a male or a female lead. I go to see a female lead as often as a male one, so why there's disparity in the pay cheque I have no idea. Bosses need to be talked to about this".

Dame Diana was honoured in Cannes for a lifetime working in TV, having most recently appeared as the Duchess of Buccleuch in ITV's Victoria. For all her many credits though, she didn't tend to watch herself on screen. "Been there, done that, all of it. Dredging up the past isn't my style. I prefer to move on".

In an episode of The Avengers from 1967, the evil, whip-swishing, megalomaniacal German movie mogul Z Z von Schnerk paid tribute to his leather-clad adversary, Emma Peel: 'You are a woman of courage, beauty and action. A woman who could become desperate, yet remain strong, become confused yet remain intelligent, who could fight back, yet remain feminine'.

Dame Diana Rigg, long unzipped but essentially the same package, continued to defend civilisation decades later, coming out in support of chivalry, declaring that women who objected to traditional courtesies like men opening doors for them were 'stupid': "If a man holds a door open for me, or pulls back a chair so that this old bag can sit down, I'm delighted. If they put an arm around a woman then say, 'You look good today', they can find themselves in court. Women who carp about that are stupid. They find it belittling, but it's just good manners".

This hadn't go down too well with everyone, The Guardian accusing Rigg of 'laying into other women', Suzanne Moore stating that the 74-year-old was a 'Gosh, I'm so successful, I don't need feminism' type. The BBC quoted a source that said that extending simple courtesies to women might indeed be 'benevolent sexism' and 'potentially harmful'.

Diana had been doubtful about the Sisterhood for decades, declaring in the '60s: "I find the whole feminist thing very boring. They are so much on the defensive that they dare not love a man, because they feel assaulted by being dependent". In prime old-bathood, the vulnerability wasn't obvious. Few actresses who'd been voted The Sexiest Woman on Television could reasonably expect to be still working in their '70s but Rigg was in strong demand, guest-starring in the Doctor Who episode 'The Crimson Horror', a title which referred to alien mischief, with her daughter Rachael Stirling.

She was also at large among the heaving bosoms, serpents and swordfights of the TV fantasy smash hit Game of Thrones, in the role of Lady Olenna Tyrell. George R R Martin, who wrote the best-selling books the show was based on, thought that casting Diana was a fantasy in itself: "She was the hottest woman on television ever, I was madly in love with her in The Avengers, along with virtually all the boys of my generation".

The Avengers, a quirkily British spy-fi series, followed the adventures of John Steed, a bowler-hatted Old Etonian special agent played by Patrick Macnee, with his glamorous-but-deadly assistant played first by Honor Blackman then from 1965 to 1967 by Rigg. The show was a hit – but it wasn't where the career of the young Diana had seemed to be heading.

She joined the programme from the Royal Shakespeare Company, where she'd triumphed as Cordelia in Peter Brook's King Lear. "If she doesn't waste herself on silly stuff, she could be quite good," concluded Brook, but his words were ignored. Rigg had never really explained why she took the role of Emma Peel, saying only that it was "a perverse decision, in a long line of perverse decisions".

She'd always been impetuous, prone to 'sudden and explosive temper', having long excelled at playing women with unsettling, obsessive characters – Mrs Danvers, the spooky housekeeper in Daphne du Maurier's Rebecca, along with the deranged Mrs Dedlock in Bleak House among them. One might trace such traits to a lonely childhood, the daughter of who Diana described as "rather Edwardian" Yorkshire parents, who took her to India at the age of two months when her father found a job as a railway engineer. She was later sent to a boarding school in Pudsey, where she "felt like a fish out of water. I was quite a loner".

Rigg felt drawn to acting, getting a place at RADA then joining the RSC soon afterwards. Her 1st marriage, during 1973, to an Israeli painter, lasted 3 years, her second, in 1982, to raffish Scottish landowner Archie Stirling, produced her only child, Rachael, but ended during 1990 after he had an affair with actress Joely Richardson. Diana lives alone, but rejects any suggestion that her life has been a disappointment. A decade earlier she sued then won, when the Daily Mail described her as an 'embittered' recluse, living by herself in France, an ungallant observation to make about a lady who'd lit up the stage for 50 years, winning awards in the West End and on Broadway. Manners mattered in the world of Dame Rigg. Take her coat, pull her up a chair, don't ask about feminism, or she might just squeeze back into the old leathers then plant a spiked heel in your nostril.

Dame Diana Rigg became a swinging '60s icon as Emma Peel in the hit spy show The Avengers then starred as the girl who became Mrs. James Bond in On Her Majesty's Secret Service. In the years since, Diana had punctuated a significant career on the London and New York stages with appearances in cult movies including The Hospital, Theater Of Blood, and The Great Muppet Caper. 50 years after becoming a TV star, she was back on television in a showy role as the scheming, sarcastic Lady Olenna in Game Of Thrones.

"Women Beware Women was black and white, and it was absolutely fascinating, because there were 3 cameras and the director had to really work out his camera placement, otherwise you'd end up with a cat's cradle in all the wires. It was exciting, because it was very sort of first-nightish. There were retakes, but you desperately tried not to have retakes. Arising out of that sort of situation, there were various wheezes that actors did if they forgot their lines.

They quite simply mouthed words silently, so it sounded as if the sound had failed then I suppose they had to go back to do it again. There was a guy called Carlos Thompson, who was I think Argentinian, who was making a series called Sentimental Agent. That was the very first thing that I did. It was supposed to be taking place in some exotic location, but in actual fact it was Chertsey with a few shivering potted palms".

Rigg had said that Harry Corbett, her leading man in The Hothouse, was 'horrible' to her.

"Yeah, he wasn't a nice person to work with. He was very, very sour, and I was replacing the director's wife. I think she'd fallen ill or something, so the director didn't like me either, because he wanted his wife. It wasn't a happy experience at all. I rose above, as one does. Women Beware Women, did you see that? It's good. That's black and white, too. It's rather splendid that they'd do a sort of Jacobean drama for television, isn't it? Fat chance of that happening now".

Had those early TV parts led to Diana being cast as Emma Peel?

"Do you know, I've no idea how I got The Avengers? I'd left the Royal Shakespeare Company, I was one of a long list of girls, but got it on my audition. We were filmed and you had to fight a stuntman. There was a stuntman called Ray Austin, and the poor man, by the time I got to him—it was about 4 in the afternoon—he'd been bashed around by so many desperate actresses, absolutely determined to get the part. He was a very sorry sight!"

The writer-producer Brian Clemens, who'd died that January, was usually mentioned as the main creative force behind The Avengers.

"Yes, he was, and very much behind all the sort of innovations of The Avengers but we did have a stellar cast of directors, who had all of them, in one way or another, like Roy Ward Baker and folk like Charlie Crichton, had made Ealing comedies and things. It was quite extraordinary. These men probably would've rather despised working in TV, but the fact of the matter was that movies, certainly English films, were in decline, so they were very glad to get a job in television, which they did brilliantly, I was very lucky to work with those sort of directors".

Did Rigg have any trouble, at the outset, capturing the unique tone of the show—that sort of droll, unflappable quality that Steel and Mrs. Peel always had?

"I sort of vaguely knew Patrick Macnee, who looked kindly on me, sort of husbanding me through the first couple of episodes. After that we became equal, loved each other and sparked off each other. We'd then improvise, write our own lines. They trusted us. Particularly our scenes when we were finding a dead body—I mean, another dead body. How do you get 'round that one? They allowed us to do it".

That's very unusual. It's hard to imagine anyone improvising dialogue on Game Of Thrones.

"Not for an instant, no. Well, when I say improvising, Pat and I would sit down to work out roughly what we'd say. It wasn't sort of... who's the American duo? Mike Nichols and Elaine May. It was definitely not that".

Was Diana still close to Patrick Macnee?

"You'll always be close to somebody that you worked with very intimately for so long, you become really fond of each other, but we haven't seen each other for a very, very long time".

When Rigg looked back on The Avengers, what did she feel about it, regarding its place in her career?

"Gratitude. That I was, having been working my way up the Royal Shakespeare Company, being with them for 5 years, starting as a walk-on then ending up as Cordelia in the Lear that played here, at Lincoln Center, with Paul Scofield. I knew that in order to develop further, I had to leave. I was lucky enough to get The Avengers but after the first season I went straight back to Stratford, to say 'Thank you' and, 'Now I can put bums on seats'. So that's what I did, doing Twelfth Night. In actual fact I doubled Twelfth Night and The Avengers. I was going backwards and forwards to Stratford. I played matinees Wednesday, matinee and evenings Saturdays, and the other days of the week I was filming in Elstree'.

Diana had obviously made a priority of the theatre. Had she made a conscious choice to put that first, ahead of a career in the movies?

"Not that I remember, no. I've never really been offered a lot of film things. I think there was a bit of a stigma in those days with TV. They thought 'overexposure', or 'too strongly associated with the character'. Who knows? If you think about it, not many people now, in America, have made good on film subsequent to television".

Rigg had starred in a number of pictures in the years right after The Avengers.

"Well, I kept on going back to the theatre, so I think the message was finally received that that was where my heart was".

The Hospital (1971)— 'Barbara Drummond'

"That's a very good movie. It's courtesy of Paddy Chayefsky that I got that part. He saw me in Abelard And Heloise, on Broadway then he fought for me to get the job. We adored each other. We used to play Scrabble when we had time. He'd put Yiddish words down on the board and I'd scream at him!".

Was Chayefsky more important to that picture than Arthur Hiller? He exercised a lot of control over the films that he wrote.

"Oh, I don't know. No. Arthur was the director, definitely. Paddy went on to write Network, he wanted me to play the Faye Dunaway part, but I didn't get it. So he called her Diana".

What was Diana's impression of George C. Scott?

"He was a very troubled man. Is he still alive? Well... He was one of those folk who rather despise themselves for being actors but I despise those sort of people. He was a brilliant actor, undoubtedly, but he was very troubled, he did disappear from time to time, for quite lengthy periods. That was when Paddy and I would hit the Scrabble board. I liked working with him hugely, because you never knew what he was going to do, and there was this sort of power emanating from him. It was, like, reined in, you never knew when it would burst. I loved it. It was very exciting, and I think our scenes were quite good. So I enjoyed the whole thing.

Julius Caesar (1970)—'Portia'

"It was all right, but it wasn't an entirely successful film at all. It was made on a shoestring. You might notice people leaning up against pillars which shake from time to time and we were all dressed in sheets. It was Charlton Heston's dream to do it and we did it, I think it was in Madrid. Jason Robards wasn't happy. He wasn't a happy bunny. He looked like Widow Twankey with those curls. He looked sort of—what's the word?—harried. Worried. 'What am I doing here?'"

On Her Majesty's Secret Service (1969)— 'Tracy'

"I enjoyed it. It was the aftermath, the fallout that just wasn't good. For either of us [Rigg and George Lazenby], actually, because it appeared as if we were scrapping, but we weren't. I very much enjoyed—I mean, it was a very luxe film. Pots of money. Lovely locations and a good script".

There's the sense that the picture is so popular among Bond fans largely because of Rigg's character, who added some emotion and gravitas to the formula.

"Yes. Unlike most Bond heroines, she had a touch of melancholy about her. She was much more substantial than most".

Had there been a lot of input from the director, Peter Hunt, or the producers in terms of that aspect of the character? Or was that something Diana brought to it?

"No, there wasn't a lot. No. That was me, fleshing it out rather more than—I mean, the way I played it. In terms of the script, I didn't add to it at all, but I knew why I was there: I was there to help George through, and to give more substance. Probably because George was completely green as an actor. He wasn't bad. He wasn't bad, at all. He was just rather difficult and temperamental to handle".

The Assassination Bureau (1969)—'Sonya Winter'

"It wasn't a good film. Basil Dearden, now there's another highly accomplished director. Absolutely wonderful. Huge string of English movies behind him. Nice man, really nice man and Telly Savalas, who was a very good actor".

It was a real star vehicle for Rigg. Oliver Reed may've been top billed, but her character was the protagonist.

"I haven't seen it. I once met an accountant who challenged me, saying, 'I put money in your film and I lost every penny!' That was The Assassination Bureau. He was a very cross little person".

Were there a lot of Diana's pictures that she hadn't seen?

"I don't actually watch myself, no. From time to time I went to see Women Beware Women, about 3 or 4 years ago. They were doing it at the Southbank when they asked me to go, I was pleasantly surprised. It was rather better than I remembered".

Rigg surely had some Oliver Reed stories.

"He was a man who liked his booze. It's sort of weird when folk who are intemperate become heroes, because there's a side of intemperance which is deeply ugly. He was rather fond of getting hold of the poor little third assistant then getting him drunk. The boy couldn't say no then he'd be on the set with a godawful hangover the following day".

Theater Of Blood (1973)—'Edwina Lionheart'

"That's a brilliant movie. I think it's so original, the characters are so wonderful. It has an implacability about it that everybody's going to get murdered at some time or another. It's a bit clunky in places but it's a wonderful idea. I think Vincent Price gives a great performance, and proves that he could've been a great classical actor, had he wanted to".

Had Diana had fun with all the disguises?

"Oh, I adored it. I mean, I wasn't terribly good as the male policeman. It was awfully hard to be a fella; it was quite hard, but all the others, I loved it. I loved working with all those folk. A great range of brilliant character actors in that film. Dennis Price was absolutely adorable. He, in his day, had been a huge heartthrob. Then there was Robert Morley, deeply eccentric, wonderful in the part, pink suit and all those poodles. There was Coral Browne, who set her sights on Vincent Price".

They'd got wed after that, hadn't they?

"Yeah, but... Vincent asked me if I'd go with him to a charity show, Cowardy Custard at the Mermaid Theatre. I went to the loo at the interval, Coral was in the next door cubicle, she suddenly said [imitating Browne's nasal drawl], 'It's a long time since I've fancied a man of my own age, but I fancy Vincent

Price'. So in the car on the way home, Vincent said, 'It's Coral's birthday next week. What can I get her?' I said, 'You have it on your person. Look no further'".

Had he not known? Was it news to him that she was interested?

"That was news to him but they were at it like knives. Two really, really very tired people on set. Coral told me they'd sat on the edge of the bed then they combined ages: 'We're 167 or something'. They'd worked it out. It was divinely funny. Anyway, it all worked out a treat. Except, that I didn't know that he was married and had a daughter. I didn't know that, otherwise I wouldn't have encouraged it. If I sound sort of po-faced, so be it".

Diana (1973-74)—'Diana Smythe'

"It was extraordinary, because they approached me. The producer [Leonard Stern] was a charming man but what I didn't know was, it was a carbon copy of The Mary Tyler Moore Show, only me being English. So it was doomed from the beginning but the fact of the matter is, Barbara Barrie, adorable woman, and Barnard Hughes, who was in The Hospital, and Richard Shull— great and we had such fun, even though we were doomed. There's nothing like being doomed to pull people together".

It seemed like Rigg was positioned as a straight actor for all those kooky characters. Was that how she'd wanted it?

"It was how it fell out. You don't have much say in the matter, frankly. I mean, I signed up for it and it was very good experience. God, learning 60 pages of dialogue / week then delivering it in front of a live audience. It was quite droll, because when I arrived they sent the limo then when I left they sent the studio station wagon. Just: Get out of town".

Extras (2006)—'Diana Rigg'

Regarding comedies, imagining them pitching that scene to Diana, when she & Daniel Radcliffe were playing themselves then she ended up with the 'Johnny' on her head...

"Well, it was an instant yes, wasn't it? Because it was beautifully written, very concise, and lovely working with Daniel, who was adorable. In fact, it took forever to film, because we were laughing so much. Every time we started, we were breaking up".

The Great Muppet Caper (1981) — 'Lady Holiday'

"I did the picture, Charles Grodin was in it as well. I don't know what was going on—something technical — Charles and I were in the scene with Miss Piggy when we had to do take after take after take then finally Charles said to me under his breath, 'Bet you never thought you'd be doing 15 takes for a f*ckin' puppet!' I did it for my daughter, who was passionately in love with Miss Piggy. She was about 5 or 6, when she came to the studio with a couple of friends to meet Miss Piggy then she burst into tears when she saw her".

From joy, or fear?

"I think she was more frightened than anything, because Miss Piggy was huge. They had several Miss Piggys. The people were lovely, Frank Oz and Jim Henson, absolutely charming, lovely people and I'd adored the show on the telly. I was a fan".

Doctor Who (2013)—'Mrs. Gillyflower'

Having survived her encounter with Miss Piggy, Rigg's daughter Rachael Stirling became an actress, mother & daughter having worked together on Doctor Who.

"Yeah, that was fun. Mark Gatiss writes a lot of that show, also writing Sherlock—very, very clever man. I worked with him on All About My Mother, which was an adaptation of the Almodovar movie, which we did onstage at the Old Vic. He was playing a transsexual, I was playing a lesbian, and we got on really well. He played with Rachael in The Recruiting Officer then became friendly with Rachie, suggesting that he write something for she and I. Which was great fun".

Too bad he hadn't got Diana into Sherlock as well.

"Yeah. Well, the women's parts in Sherlock aren't that great, are they?"

What was the best woman's role in Shakespeare?

"Probably Cleopatra".

Rigg played her onstage in Antony And Cleopatra.

"Not terribly well. I just ... it didn't work. First of all, the set was a b*gger. It was grey. It had to double for Rome and Egypt, with the bias in Rome. Those huge grey columns were just not Egyptian at all. No sense of sunlight, heat, luxury and Cleopatra. I'm not blaming the set. I'm saying it was part of the reason that the thing didn't work. Obviously performances are the main reasons. I just wasn't happy and I just didn't find her".

King Lear (1983)— 'Regan'

What had it been like to play opposite Laurence Olivier as Lear?

"We were all there to pay homage to him. He'd never done it, and he was ill. I was a replacement for Faye Dunaway. She'd worked with the director, Michael Elliott, a lot before then suddenly, I don't know how, I was asked to do it. Michael was tetchy with me for some reason I simply couldn't understand. I think he'd worked so closely with Faye Dunaway, having this image of exactly how he wanted Regan to be played.

It was about the third day into rehearsal when he was on me again, Olivier said, 'Leave her alone. She knows what she's doing'. He wanted to do all those speeches in one take, because he wished to approximate what would happen on stage but he couldn't do it. It was agony, agony watching him force himself. He never got through any of the speeches. They had to be cut together".

A Midsummer Night's Dream (1968)— 'Helena'

Diana was in this film version with Helen Mirren and Judi Dench. What were they like at that age?

"Oh, like they are now, but young. Very good, but young. It was a very uncomfortable experience. It was Warwickshire in November. It was incredibly cold. I didn't think I'd ever hear a director saying this, but I had this little slip of a cotton dress on, so I bought some woolly knickers to wear underneath. I didn't know it at the time, but the angle of the camera—I was up a tree, when I heard Peter Hall say, 'Diana, take your knickers off!'"

Game Of Thrones (2013-17)— 'Lady Olenna'

The show was produced on several continents. Where had Rigg shot her scenes?

"They're in Belfast, or Dubrovnik".

Where was Lady Olenna's garden?

"Dubrovnik. It's beautiful, lovely. I think it must've belonged to some aristocratic family or something, it's got these pergolas and walks, it's just ravishing. It's on a cliff, overlooking the sea".

One by one, Diana had had a scene with all the great character actors in the cast.

"It's wonderful working with them, because quite a lot of them I've worked with before. Charles Dance I've worked with before, Julian Glover I've worked with before, in the theatre. You pick up the threads with them again after many years, it's lovely that for the most part, there are a lot of English actors. Mind you, I think we pitch up. We know our lines. We don't demand 60-ft Winnebagos and we're grateful".

A few months earlier Rigg's only comment on Game Of Thrones had been 'they do write some rather good lines for me, don't they?'

"Yeah, they do. I think they've got my measure as an actress, they write for that, which is great!"

Diana had some good directors on Game Of Thrones, Michelle MacLaren directing one of her episodes.

"Yeah, she was great. I love being directed. Folk think when you're established that you come on with all guns blazing and you're not open, but I love being directed, because it's another thought, it's another fresh idea. You're so grateful for an original idea that you haven't had".

Rigg had a Tony, along with a 'Dame' in front of her name. Had she ever found that directors were intimidated by her?

"I hope not. I'd be horrified if they were".

Who were the best directors Diana had worked with?

"John Dexter, who was at the Met here in New York for a long time. He was a demanding man, very demanding. His career was quite extraordinary. He commissioned a Phaedra for me, we did Pygmalion together then we did The Misanthrope together, which played Broadway. John was very honest. I remember he could be very cruel, a fact that I didn't like, obviously but he had an overall view.

The thing I absolutely hate is when directors don't know what they want, but then they ask you to do it this way then maybe that way, maybe that way, because they haven't made up their minds what they want. So you're running around in circles trying to give them what they want, for me it's really bad news, because I get bored with listening to myself and I get tetchy with them for not knowing".

It sounded like Rigg was describing someone in particular.

"I was, actually, but I'm not going to mention names".

Dexter directed Diana onstage. Who were some of the best movie directors she'd worked with?

"I loved Arthur Hiller. He was great but I can't speak from much experience, really... I vote for the Oscars, so I see an awful lot of films. Clint Eastwood's pretty good; I loved his American Sniper. You could be in safe hands with him. I think Quentin Tarantino is absolutely fascinating. I'd love to work with him but I believe he's quite testy".

Tarantino seemed to shoot a lot of footage then find the picture in the editing room. So one might end up in that scenario Rigg had just described.

"Hmm. Yes. I'd rather not then".

It was almost exactly 50 years ago that Diana had started shooting The Avengers. How was it different being a TV star now compared to then?

"Nowadays it's not film, it's tape for TV. If you're shooting something, and I remember this with The Avengers, you'd rehearse a lot then get it, build up to the point where you're using film for a take and it's very special. When the director says 'Action', you're very heightened. Film meant something. Tape doesn't. Tape's cheap".

Game Of Thrones was shot on tape?

"Exactly. I had this conversation with the cameraman on Game Of Thrones. There's not quite that heightened sense. The kids, the younglings, know that if they're playing a scene but they forget their lines, they just pause. Nobody cuts anything. They just pause then speak again. If you're on film, that's undreamt of. It's very definitely different".

Was Rigg going to be back for the 6th season?

'I don't think I'm allowed to say!"

Off the record, was there an episode coming up that one should time this piece to?

"I'm sorry, I can't tell you, because I don't know. I haven't seen any scripts. They're held very close to their chests".

Diana hadn't already shot a juicy death scene or something...?

"Oh, you're expecting me to die?"

Well, they'd kept Rigg on past her character's last appearance in the books, hadn't they?

"I know. I'm on life support!"

58

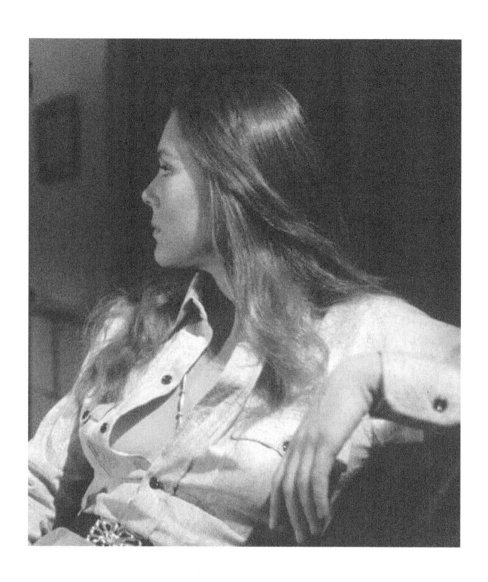

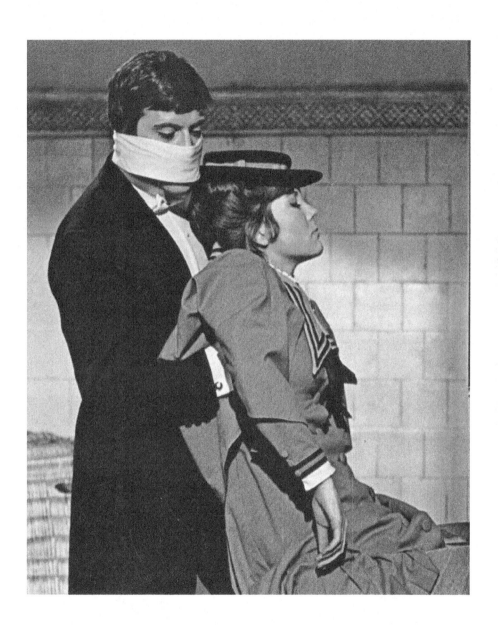

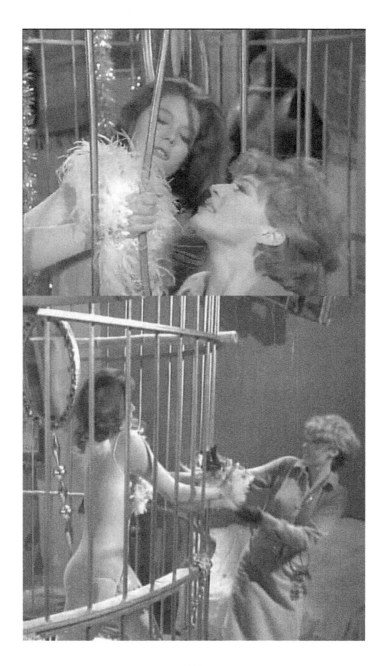

117

133

140

155

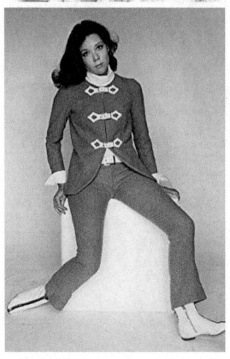

161

161

Made in the USA
Las Vegas, NV
26 February 2021

18274874R10095